AF411675

To Follow a Dream

"And he dreamed, and behold a ladder set up on the earth, and the top of it reached to heaven . . . And, behold, the Lord stood above it, and said, I am the Lord . . . I am with thee, and will keep thee."
Genesis 28:12-15

To Follow A Dream
Donald McKinney

BROADMAN PRESS
Nashville, Tennessee

Dewey Decimal Classification: 242
Subject heading: DEVOTIONAL LITERATURE

Library of Congress Catalog Card Number: 79-51999
Printed in the United States of America.

To Virginia Griffis, in memory of
her father, Lee Outland, a great
educator who made it possible for
a boy to go to college by awarding
him a scholarship

Preface

No Christian reading the twenty-first chapter of the Gospel of John can help the deep feeling of pity that comes into his heart as Simon Peter stands before Jesus Christ and listens to the words "Feed my sheep."

At sometime in life each one of us has sat in a corner and cried our heart out from deep sorrow and we can feel the pain in the life of the man who denied Jesus. What a just thing it would have been for Jesus to condemn Peter, but instead Jesus said, "I love you and I need you—feed my sheep."

Today that same voice of Jesus speaks to your heart. Do you realize each day what you do to feed Christ's sheep? People have thrilled to your words coming over the telephone on a morning that started out to be ordinary to them, "I have been thinking about you," or "I wanted to talk to you," or "I miss you."

And have you thought lately of a friend in a faraway city who opened your letter with trembling fingers and read your words, "I wanted you to have this before Christmas. I hope you are happy. I think of you so often." What you are saying is, "I love you. I love you because of all you have been to me and my family." And you know that you wrote it because the living Christ is living in your heart today.

It was the birthday of the world when the angels sang over the hills of Bethlehem "Joy to the world, a Saviour is born." Jesus came to tell us of God's unending forgiveness and love and promise of eternal life. *To Follow a Dream* is about you because you have been there so many times to touch and to lift a life that has faced defeat. Jesus instilled in the lives of all he touched a sense of individual importance and the ability to grow.

To Follow a Dream is to give purpose to life. In recent times the art of looking up has been replaced by the opposite. News reporting and fiction writing have become negative and depressing. High moral standards are ignored. It is time to lift our heads again, to recapture the lost art of looking up.

If you have sometimes felt life closing in on you, if your faith grows dim, this book will renew your faith in God and in yourself. These are real people who have chosen to serve Jesus Christ no matter how dark the valley. And because of their deep faith, they have hoped and lived again.

Contents

The Gift of Yourself

"Take of the best fruits in the land in your vessels,
and carry down the man a present, a little balm,
and a little honey."

Genesis 43:11

The most cherished Christmas present I ever received was a box of cookies and candy. Thank you Barbara Johnson. The plain, gray box had been covered with gay wrapping paper. The card was cut from an old Christmas card. The candy and cookies she had made, working late into the night after her teaching day ended. Everything was homemade. It seemed to say, "This is a part of me."

You have given away so many things you have made with your hands—a mess of carrots you dug from your garden, a knitted sweater, or your time to work as a volunteer in a hospital. All say, "This is a part of me."

A child said one Christmas morning, "Grandpa, I found an apple for me under the tree with a ten-dollar bill tied to it. It was from Santa Claus. Is that you?"

He pulled her upon his knee and put his arm around her shoulder. "Well, if Santa Claus brought it, I wouldn't ask any questions. No one really ever gives you anything. Whatever you get you have earned."

How true were his words. He was thinking of the childhood laughter in his home. Of her visits to his house when she brought cookies and pies her mother had baked. Of a kiss on his cheek when she left.

Dr. Harry Leeds left one of his most loved paintings to an eighteen-year-old girl. She was no relation to him but had admired the picture one time when attending a Sunday School party in the doctor's home. He said to me, "I decided to give her the painting because of what she did for me. One Sunday morning the church steps were slick with ice and I was afraid of falling. She came running out the church door, held my arm tightly, and helped me down the steps to my car." Yes, anyone could have done that. And so, he remembered her.

I walked into a hospital room one afternoon while working as a volunteer to take a patient to physical therapy. "Yes," the woman said, noting the look of disbelief on my face, "there are two hundred and ten cards pasted on the wall. I am getting about ten a day. I'm just a nurse here in the hospital. I slipped and broke my leg Monday."

Just a nurse with a broken leg. How her gentleness and love must have reached out to others. There is so much good in all of us. You are special in so many lives. People remember forever your smile and your kindness. Sometimes it takes a stay in a hospital to remind us of long-forgotten friends.

When Israel asked that his sons take a little honey to Joseph in Egypt, he was sending a rare and cherished sweet. It was something extra that he wanted to give. It goes back to the very beginning—the gift of ourselves.

When you give yourself, you give that something special like a box of homemade cookies or a knitted sweater or a bunch of carrots.

I Light My Candle

You cannot wait to hold your candle before the world tomorrow. You must do it today. To be needed is a gift from God. It comes to you because you are a child of God's, an heir to eternal life. How thrilling are the words of Jesus.

When William Kempter called me last night and said, "We need you to serve on the board of the Boy's Club," I began to make excuses. "My time is limited. Others can do a better job. I don't know anything about the work."

There was silence at the other end of the line. I thought my excuses were all good. Then the thought came to me—how many people has he called who gave him the same excuses I did? Or, maybe he called me first because he felt I had something to give. Perhaps he called me because he wanted me.

"Something to give!" What do we really give to the needs of others? Well, we give our money, our time, ourselves. Do we? Or do we just give what we don't need? How much is a boy worth? I must mow my grass. I must wash the car. I must help with the dishes, sometimes with the cooking. I must work at my job to pay my bills. Does life have more meaning than all of these?

I looked down my quiet street of substantial houses. I thought of my town with its good fire and police protection and the waterworks, and the parks. Was I overlooking something more valuable? Who builds Boy Scout camps? Who leads a day camp for the Girl's Club? Who works with Meals on Wheels? Who serves on the school board? Who takes a neighbor to a doctor?

All of us carry a light. Sometimes we feel like a showoff. We fear that someone will say, "Oh, he just wants to see his name in the paper." Sometimes the light is reflected back, and we begin to realize how great a person we are. Mrs. Jones had to be coaxed into taking her turn being a den mother. "I'll do it for the children," she said reluctantly. She found it was fun and rewarding. The children needed her and they loved her.

It does not take much time to carry a candle. It can be done with a telephone call or a get-well card. You can send someone singing on his way with seven magic words, "We missed you at the meeting yesterday."

We don't need to compete with God. His candle comes up shining brightly in the morning on our cabbage and beans. Ours can light a life with the simple words, "Good morning," or "Thank you."

To be needed is really a gift from God. When Jesus said that man was the light of the world, he was saying for all time that every living person is worthy of being loved—has something unique to give to the world.

Peter and John had no gold to give to the sick man at the Gate Beautiful. They asked him to lift his eyes and to look up and to get up. When he did, he became a man with a heart filled with joy. Look up, lift your candle—which means to give yourself today in order that you may know the warmth within your heart of caring for another.

I Do Not Call One Greater

"Who is the greatest in the Kingdom of heaven?"
Matthew 18:1

Sometimes we put man in little cubicles. We get his number, so to speak, by the kind of car he drives, the kind of house he lives in, the clothes he wears, the degrees he has from colleges, the clubs he belongs to, the job he does.

Walt Whitman once wrote words that have endured the years, "I do not call one greater and one smaller. That which fills its period and place is equal to any." Do we really believe this? Jesus does. He said that any person as humble as a little child is the greatest in the kingdom.

Will Harris said to me, "I treat with deep respect the man who fixes my TV, the woman who puts the food on my tray when I am in the hospital, the boy who rakes the leaves in my yard."

Mildred Sanders paid special attention to the children who came into her classroom in September and selected seats at the back of the room. Once I heard her say to a boy who had been kicked out of English class by a teacher, "Now, Charles, I want you to feel welcome in my room. I am glad to have you. I want to help you have a happy year. I hope you and I can be friends." This was the way Jesus talked to the unhappy, the discouraged, the shunned of his day.

Miss Sanders would never have said, "Now, Charles, the teachers have all warned me about you. You are lazy, a troublemaker, and I'm going to be watching you. Just one smart-aleck trick and out you go." Like Jesus Christ, she saw in every child what he *could* become with faith, kindness, and guidance. It was her job to take the raw boy and turn him into a boy with self-respect for himself.

To have a second chance! Charles began to recite, to comb his hair, to put his hand up, to ask for a desk closer to the front of the room. We respond like Charles when we feel down and out and when in the stillness of a walk or from our pillow we hear the voice of God saying, "I believe in you. I love you. Try one more time."

Sometimes a quiet person has much to give. And you may be that one who reaches out and leads him into a field of giving. My new neighbor lived next door for six months before I met him. He was busy all the time, and I didn't want to be a bother. One day my lawnmower stopped near the fence where he was working in his garden. He knew all about small motors and fixed the mower. We talked for two hours about dogs and I found a wonderful friend.

Walt Whitman understood human nature well. He saw men employed at simple tasks, yet happy and proud of their work. The shoe cobbler prided himself on a new shoe; the baker had pride in the loaves he baked; the housewife was proud of her sewing of a new dress.

I met a man once driving a taxi in New York. We found much to talk about. He had an engineering degree and said he had never been as happy as he was driving a taxi, working out of doors, meeting and talking to people who had traveled all over the world. He enjoyed driving his taxi.

To Reach for a Dream

"The kingdom of heaven is like unto a merchant
man, seeking goodly pearls: Who, when he had
found one pearl of great price, went and sold
all that he had and bought it."
Matthew 13:45–46

The time to reach for a dream is now. Yesterday is gone,
tomorrow may never come, but we have this moment. Seven
years ago Carl Fleming enrolled in a night school. He left
school at the end of the eighth grade to help support his
six brothers and sisters. When his two children enrolled in
college, he promised them he would go back and get a high
school education. In addition to his job that earned income
for living and his duties as a husband and a father, he spent
three nights a week in night school to earn his diploma.

Is it beyond your dream to try today for something that
you missed yesterday? A boy said to me, "I can't go to college
today because I don't have the five-thousand dollars it takes."
And he added, "It didn't cost much when my father went
to college back in the thirties'."

"Yes," I said. "It cost just as much. Your father had eleven
dollars in his pocket when he packed his trunk and left for
college. He washed dishes three times a day for fifty-five boys
in a fraternity house. This paid for his meals. He lived in a
small attic room free for firing the furnace of an apartment
house, getting up at two o'clock in the morning in cold weather
to keep the soft Indiana coal alive. He waited tables. He
washed enough windows to reach around the world if they
were laid end to end. He received twenty-five cents an hour.
You can earn from two to three dollars an hour, eight to
twelve times as much as he earned."

Esther Wadsworth settled for business college in the

thirties. When she was sixty-five, a widow with married children and grandchildren, she enrolled in college. She had pounded a typewriter many years to get her children through college. Going to college at sixty-five was not easy. She doubted her ability to keep up with the teenagers. She worked part of the time in the college library, coaxed her old car to start in cold weather, and won her diploma.

She stepped into a new world. The younger students had welcomed her. Her professors were proud of her. She carried on a one-woman campaign to get the state to offer free tuition in state colleges to senior citizens. She appeared on TV. She urged others to go back to school. Once she said, "And to think that I once considered sitting in a rocker before my TV when I reached sixty-five and dying slowly on my small Social Security payment."

What is your dream? If you are a nurse, a farmer, a teacher, or a builder, God needs you in so many parts of the world. New nations need your age and experience. If you feel you have missed something in your life, the world beckons to you in faraway lands. The best years of your life can be after sixty-five. Reach for a dream.

But My Sorrow Is Different

"This sickness is not unto death, but for the glory of God."

John 11:4

I sat in the waiting room of the doctor's office. She had been afraid to go alone. I shall never forget the defeat, the tears in her eyes as my hand closed over hers. The blood sample diagnosis—suffering from pernicious anemia, a disease that reaches out to every organ of the body because not enough red corpuscles mature in the bone marrow to sustain life.

Two weeks later a letter came from her. She wrote: "I have had marvelous blessings, tempered by many traumatic and heartbreaking episodes all through my life. The heartbreaks have tried my faith over and over which was meant to be. But in the end my faith in God, my heavenly Father and Creator, has been unshaken. I intend it to remain so."

Once she had said to me, "I love my fellowmen and will do all I can to help when trouble appears." I told her one morning after church service, "Volunteer work ought to be your middle name." She was active in the volunteer drives for the kidney fund. She had been a leader for twenty-five years in the drive for the heart fund. She had been a teacher in the downtown slums of Cincinnati, collected for the Settlement House, collected food for, and worked with underprivileged children, teaching them music and art and dancing.

She *is* a remarkable woman. Her only child, a beautiful, sensitive, joyous daughter died of a brain tumor at age seven. She understands what an effort it was for Jesus to carry his cross. Life nailed her to a cross, yet she dared to live again. She said to me as we left the burial grounds, "She was such a lovely spirit with a beautiful face and beautifully porportioned body, loved by everyone who knew her, adored by her father and me." She carries another cross: "My husband is bitter. He has become a different person, drained of all desire to live. He tries, but without heart, feeling that all his plans and hard work have gone down the drain. I pray that someday there will come a crack in his closed door and he can fight his way back to life."

This is her story. How many times we fall, and sometimes it is so hard to get back up again. An elderly man's life was explained by a note found in his Bible, "I have made up my mind when I grow old not to be a grouch because the devil loves an old grouch. I don't want the devil to love me. I want God to love me."

He suffered greatly in and out of hospitals during his last years. When he died, the people lined up on the sidewalk to get into the funeral home to pay their last respects.

Yes, sometimes you do feel that your sorrow is different. We do feel a sickness unto death. But out of this sickness can come a glory as Jesus said. It is through suffering that we become worth something to others. And reaching out in fellowship to those who suffer as we have suffered, we find a comfort and peace in our hearts that shows us we do not walk through life alone.

She Is the Greatest of All

"By the way they had disputed among themselves,
who should be the greatest."
Mark 9:34

During a vacation trip in the summer of 1975, I was in
the neighborhood of a retired teacher who had taught in my
school for many years. I left the freeway and drove up a
narrow blacktop road for several miles. It eventually turned
into a gravel road thick with dust, wound along a river, and
stopped before a mailbox with the name of Rosella Branson.

Not far up the hillside was a rambling two-story frame
house of about 1840 vintage, the color long faded. A milk
goat grazed on the hillside yard and a few chickens were
around the front porch. I got out of my car and walked slowly
up the hill, keeping my eyes on what seemed to be a vicious
dog. I heard a door open and slam and a tall gray woman
stepped out and grabbed the collar of the dog.

"Yes, what is it? What do you want?" Then her manner
changed, "Why, it's my old principal." Her lips spread in a
smile as she brushed the hair out of her face and untied
the soiled apron that covered the front of her unpressed dress.

It had been ten years since I had seen Rosella Branson.
As I looked at her walking down the hillside with her hand
outstretched, I saw her only as the young woman who came
into my office one day forty years before. I remembered her
beautiful brunette hair, sparkling eyes, and musical voice. She
always wore smooth nylons, dainty slippers, a fresh tailored
dress, and a smile. She was one of my most loved teachers,
a joy to be around. I remembered how the children crowded
around her desk at recess and at noon to talk to her. She

planned games for them to play.

She demanded a fair day's work for a fair grade. She stayed after school to help a child having difficulty with arithmetic or reading. Her children felt free to come to her with their problems. She used to say, "There are no problem children, only children with problems."

I held her hand for a long time. There were so many memories to recall. She invited me into her threadbare kitchen with its wood-burning stove. She was apologetic, "I only keep two rooms open. Saves fuel in winter. I don't entertain. My brother and his family come over. They live two miles away. He farms my land."

But I didn't see the two unkept rooms, not really. I only saw the woman who was so busy teaching for forty-three years that she never had time to marry and have a family of her own. I felt it wasn't right for her to be living in the old house. She had an ample pension and could have gone to a retirement home where there would be other teachers and comfort and social life.

In September that fall I got out the last record book of Rosella Branson and went down the list of names. Out of that last class she taught, a girl and two boys were in medical school, two boys were going to be lawyers, others in training to be teachers, four in nursing school. I understood as I looked at the check for $4,000 that had come in the morning mail from an anonymous donor. A check for this amount had been coming for ten years for college scholarships—for her children.

Please Touch Me

"He put his hands again upon his eyes, and made
him look up: and he was restored."
Mark 8:25

"You know for some old folks who live alone, the church
is the only place they can get hugged." I overheard Carol
Beals say these words to a friend in the hallway of the First
Friends Church following the service one morning.

Yes, this is a good way to describe the nature of Christian
fellowship. The presence of God is always warmly felt in a
church. It is a time when the tension and stress of life, of a
job, can be pushed aside. There is a sense of loving fellowship
for others, knowing that we are surrounded by people who
know the healing power of touch.

Jesus Christ was always touching people. He touched with
his presence, with his words, with his love, with his hands.
A mother does this, a father, a friend. Looking out the window
of my house one day, I saw a small boy fall from his swing.
He got up and looked around. Then he ran around the house
to where his mother was hanging clothes on a line. The moment he saw her he began to cry. No use to cry when no
other person was around to hear. The boy's mother picked
him up in her arms and kissed him and held him tightly.
That was all he wanted, someone to know, someone to care.

When I get the blues, a hurried trip to a nursing home,
to a hospital, or an apartment where someone lives alone,
brings healing. You are like me. Your telephone, your cards,
your visits bring healing to others because you have a special
touch that "makes others look up."

People seem to know. Betty Reagan, a twenty-four-year-old, third-grade teacher said, "When I went to school last Monday I wasn't feeling good. I had problems and was really down on the world. Before the last bell rang, three of my girls had come in and put their arms around me. How did they know I needed them? When they touched me I became a person again. Their eyes and their touch told me I was no longer alone."

Many years ago I taught square dancing one summer in the big gym of the Richmond State Hospital. The men sat on one side of the gym and the women sat on the other side. The minute I said, "Get your partners," the elderly people "raced" across the floor to get a partner. The unsmiling, sad faces, suddenly lighted up as the music began and the lonely life of the institution was forgotten in the fast-stepping squares. One woman said to me, "I mark off the days with my pencil to the Saturday we will come back for another square dance."

When Jesus put his hands upon the eyes of a man and made him look up, we are told that the man was restored. How many times today have you restored faith, given courage, lifted a unhappy person to his feet again? Have you really thought about it? Doesn't it make you feel warm and thankful inside that you were there when God needed you?

Love Is a Blessing

> "I will not let thee go, except thou bless me.
> Thy name shall be called no more Jacob, but
> Israel: for as a prince hast thou power with God
> and with men."
>
> Genesis 32:26, 28

To have love in your heart is proof that you are living. When you can no longer love, you are no longer living. Love can never be a sin. It can only be a blessing. The heart dies if it loses its capacity to love.

You have seen a small girl love her doll. You have seen a boy gather his puppy in his arms and love it and talk to it. You have seen shaking hands tenderly weed the soil in a rose bed. These are acts of love.

Someone has said that no man stands so tall as when he stoops to lift another. Jacob learned that he had within him the power to be great because God loved him. So many people have achieved success and happiness in life because others have believed in them and cheered from the sidelines when the going was rough.

I heard a woman singing one night as I walked down the hall of an office building. She was on her knees mopping steps with a brush. My first thought was, "What does she have to sing about?" I learned she had a son to sing about.

"My son, William, is starting his second year in college. His father is dead. He is a good boy. He is doing well in college. He is going to be a clergyman. I am glad that my job pays enough to keep him in college. I am so proud of him."

I stepped out into the street with the many others who were going home to warm houses and evening meals, but I couldn't get the picture of her out of my mind—on her knees mopping floors for a boy who would someday stand behind a pulpit and proclaim the gospel of the love of Jesus Christ. He would be there because of a mother who loved him. And his work would bless so many people in the many years to come.

I watched a nurse put her arm around the shoulders of an old man to help him sit up in the hospital bed. When I mentioned her kindness to him, she said, "Oh, he doesn't have anyone who comes to see him. He reminds me of my father. I hope someone will do that for my father when he is old."

Thomas Chalmers served as pastor of a little church in Scotland. He was not very successful. No one ever came to the altar although he preached hellfire and eternal suffering to his poor men and women who came from the stony farms to hear him.

One Sunday morning at the little church in Kilmany a simple farmer said to him: "You preach to us as though we lived in a week of sin. We are simple people trying to keep food in our mouths."

Thomas Chalmers changed his life because a simple man spoke to him. Chalmers began to pour from his pulpit the truth of the eternal love of Jesus Christ and the altar was filled. He went on to become a distinguished economist and author and professor of divinity at the University of Edinburgh. And all because a simple man taught him that it is only in loving our fellowmen that we lift them to the glory of God.

Abraham Lincoln, the Dreamer

"And Joseph dreamed a dream."
Genesis 37:5

The Lincoln Memorial in Washington, D. C., has been called one of the most handsome memorials of this century. A majestic statue of the Great Emancipator fills the west wall. The statue has been looked upon by millions of school children, Americans, and foreign visitors.

Lincoln believed in a democratic government. He believed that God intended no man to be a slave to another man. The true greatness in Lincoln lies in what he was. He was poor as were many boys in his day. He became president of the United States because he prepared himself for greatness. He had a dream; and he followed his dream, slaying the giants that got in his way—the lack of public schools and the smallness of opportunity, the need to make a living with his hands, his failure again and again at the work he tried.

Lincoln did not want to be a rail-splitter all his life. He was not handsome, and he made fun of himself in order to be able to live with himself. He rose to greatness because he believed that he could, not because opportunity lay before him.

I knew Wendell M. Stanley when he played football for Morton High School in Richmond, Indiana. Most people knew him as a football player. He graduated from Earlham College where he was known as a football player. But his real love was the laboratory where he came under the influence of Ernest A. Wildman, a man he later spoke of as "a splendid teacher of chemistry."

Wendell M. Stanley was an ordinary boy who lived down a side street in Richmond, a boy who played football. But he went on to the University of California; won the Nobel prize in chemistry; became a member of the Rockefeller Institute of Medical Research, famous for its study of the viruses; and has a science hall at Earlham College named after him.

Like Abraham Lincoln, Wendell Stanley had to work his way to the top. He was not a rich boy. But somewhere along the way, a great teacher at Earlham touched his life and he knew what he wanted to become. He became one of the greatest in science.

We do not have to have rich parents. We do not have to be born in a big city. We do not have to be first in our class to find success in life. We have to have a dream. Maybe *you* are the person who gave a boy or a girl a dream. It is what a person has on the inside—courage, faith, a desire—that leads that person to overcome all obstacles to reach a goal.

Of all the brothers, Joseph is the only one who is really remembered. He is remembered for the qualities of his life that made it possible to reach the top. He was wise, yes. But he was forgiving, understanding, compassionate, and felt a deep sense of duty towards his fellowmen. He lived to make the world around him better.

Remember Who You Are

"Ask, and it shall be given you; seek, and ye shall
find; knock, and it shall be opened unto you."
Matthew 7:7

Do you love the work you do? Do you feel the importance
of what you do? Fred Emerson is a truck driver. It is hard
work, and he is away from home on weekends. He has every
Thursday off, however, and he has become a volunteer worker
in the city hospital on Thursday afternoon.

Fred tells his story: "I get a chance to talk to lonely people,
people who are frightened, people who hurt, people who worry
about their jobs and their families. People find it hard to
adjust when suddenly pushed out of the kitchen, the office,
or the shop into a hospital bed. There they are surrounded
by strangers and are dependent on strangers for every need."

Fred is like many—working at trucking—a job he does
not like, but one that makes him a good living. Now he is
learning the joy of walking the second mile, doing something
without pay for others that gives him self-satisfaction. "A
whole new life has opened for me," Fred said. "I learned
about this hospital volunteer work one Sunday morning when
I was pounding down the highway from Pittsburg. I had tuned
in on a church service like I always do on Sunday, and I
got the idea from the sermon."

Fred knows his truck moves vital goods needed by people.
He has a job to do and does it. When you see a dishwasher
in a restaurant, a man at the gasoline pumps, a bus driver,
or a farmer, don't assume they are unhappy at their jobs.
Many people don't like to work but find happiness in rendering
services and goods needed by others.

Mrs. Flemming said to me one morning, "I like to wash dishes. Some women don't. I admire the craftsmanship that goes into the making of a plate or a glass. I am happy to have hot water coming out of a faucet into my pan, for I used to carry water from a pump when I was a child. I like to stack clean dishes in my cupboard. Of course there are other things I enjoy, but I have no complaint about the jobs that must be done daily."

A dentist said: "I get tired looking into mouths day after day. But it is a great satisfaction to me to know that my work helps a person. I know how important his smile is, and I am happy to help him keep good teeth."

An elderly woman said, "I don't work anymore and people think I am alone and never see people. That isn't so. I always find some nice greeting for the clerk at the post office, for the girl who takes my money when I pay my utility bills, for the boy who sacks my groceries in the supermarket."

We have only to ask. We have only to seek. We have only to knock. The door will be opened, but God asks us to do something. And when we do, he is waiting to answer our need.

Good Morning to You

"The heavens declare the glory of God."
Psalm 19:1

What you say or think when you first awaken can set the entire mood of your day. The negative person may say: "Here it is another morning. Have to get up and dress and get my breakfast and fix my hair and wash the dishes and go to work."

You can change your life by becoming a positive person. This kind of person says: "I am glad to be alive at the beginning of a new day. I am going to see two new beautiful things. I am going to speak to three strangers and make new friends. I am going to lift my eyes to the heavens and thrill with this wonderful, wonderful world and its people."

Mrs. Means said one morning: "It is so lonesome to live alone. I came to this house sixty-five years ago. All the people I used to know are gone. I've outlived them all. And the people on this road! Go in any direction and they are all newcomers." She picked up her knitting. "I remember when I used to visit back and forth on the telephone, but I don't know anybody now."

"How well do you know Jeanie Reeves who lives in the red brick down the road?"

"Oh, I haven't met her. Been meaning to call her on the phone and make an appointment to stop, but never got it done. She is so busy."

"Why don't you just stop in?"

"Oh, I couldn't do that. He's a doctor you know, and she is a nurse. They are such busy people."

But Mrs. Means did stop in. She found Mrs. Reeves wanted

to learn to knit and Mrs. Means taught her. And later on when I met Mrs. Means again, she said to me: "You know, I got around to calling on all the young folks who have moved into the neighborhood. They are all such nice people and do the most interesting things. I don't think I'll ever be lonesome again."

People are important to people. On a recent trip to Russia I learned to say just two words in Russian—thank you! Wherever I went, the word *spasibo* called forth a smile from people who do not smile too much. They were pleased that I had taken the time to learn that much of their language.

Try saying good morning to the person on the elevator, to the person you hold a door open for, to the waitress, to the policeman. A smile and a cheerful thought goes far to making for a happy day.

The psalmist lifted his eyes to the skies. The sky is never the same. But from early morning until late in the afternoon, God puts on a celestial show, sometimes with all the colors of the rainbow. The rising sun and the lighting up of the world is his way of saying: "I am the Lord, your God. Good morning to you. Have a good day."

Someone Remembers You

A letter came this morning from a woman who is thirty-two years of age and the mother of three children. She writes:

"It seems that God works in ways that we never quite understand. He seems to know all about what our lives will become. When I was a senior in high school, my parents got a divorce. I remember all too well the trying and very horrible weeks that followed. A certain teacher kept me in after class one day. He kindly asked me about my horrible disposition.

"I was angry at the world. I felt the world was laughing at me for something I could not change. Many adjustments had to be made, and I was rebelling against those things because hurt took over.

"This teacher told me that he did understand how I felt. And through our conversation he made me feel that there was a future and that I was fully responsible for *my* future. God had his hand on my life then. He had placed one of his servants as my teacher.

"You once told me that I was responsible for how my life turned out. I could be bitter or I could turn the event around and learn from it. My future was up to me.

"I have always been thankful that the teacher took time to ask about my circumstances at home. He cared and was willing to help and God used him as a guide for me. No one else reached out to me and frankly pointed out the road I must go, what I must do for myself.

"I have been told that each one of us will influence the lives of seven people during our lifetime. That means there are seven people who will have great influence on my life. I have so far met three of these seven people. And for years I have known that you are one of these."

What does one say when he lays a letter like this one down? Often we are not aware at the time of our influence in helping another person. It is God who gives to us a sensitive heart. It often comes through suffering. God uses us as a channel of his love to reach out to people in need. We have only to listen to God's voice, and he will tell us what to do.

Jesus was always asking questions. He was interested in people. People have not changed in heart from the day of Jesus. We are surrounded by people willing to unburden their hearts to one who cares. A friend is one who understands us, listens to us, gives us guidance, but never condemns us. When we were children, we ran to our mothers when in trouble. They were on our side. As adults, often we must bear our problems only with God because we fear to share with someone who may not understand our need. It is time for each one of us to remember anew, "As ye would that men should do to you, do ye also to them likewise." (Matt. 7:12).

Please Hold Me

"A new commandment I give unto you, That
ye love one another; as I have loved you."
John 13:34

A number of years ago a Girl Scout troop went to a mental hospital to put on a Christmas party in a children's ward. The girls took a tree, presents, candy, cookies, sandwiches, and hot chocolate. Following the distribution of gifts and the picnic lunch, the children all gathered around an old upright piano for singing.

But what I remember most of all was the blue-eyed girl, about eleven years old, who came up to me and said, "Please hold me." How sad that a child must ask to be held. I had a Santa Claus suit on. She sat on one of my knees and I put my arm around her shoulder. Within seconds another girl was on the other knee. They laid their heads on my shoulders and seemed so happy to be held. I thought of the many wonderful people who visit these unfortunate children and reach out to touch and to hold them.

Before leaving we walked through the dormitory where the children slept. The beds were just three feet apart. There were big stuffed animals on almost every bed.

Tears came into the eyes of an attendant when I asked her the question, "Is there someone here to tuck these children in at night?"

"We try to give them as much love as we can," she said. "There just aren't enough of us to go around. Some of these children can't remember a father or mother. Some of them have a parent or parents who come to visit, but most of them have no one."

As we said farewell at the door, the children begged the group to come back sometime. The Scouts picked up the smaller children and hugged them, and the older children reached out to touch the girls.

How heartwarming were the words of the attendant: "A lot of groups come here every week from churches, schools, and clubs. Women come in all during the week and play games with them and talk to them. You just wouldn't believe the love that busy people have to share with these children. There are so many good people in the world."

Not all children in need of love are in institutions. They live down the streets of every town. Sometimes they roam the streets after dark, sometimes they become vandals fighting back against a society that won't let them work, won't let them have a normal home. The schools, the teenage centers, the athletic programs, just don't seem to be enough. Yet no society in the world has cared as much and spent so much to give children a place to grow.

Peter Pan

"Suffer the little children to come unto me, and
forbid them not: for of such is the kingdom of
God."

Mark 10:14

Do you sometimes feel that you have lost the glow of childhood? Life is so demanding—your children, your job, society! To stay young in heart is the secret of facing each new day with anticipation.

Sir James Barrie got his idea for the book about Peter Pan while he was watching children playing in Kensington Gardens, England, one lazy afternoon. Peter Pan was a little person who never grew up. Sir George Frampton made the sculpture of Peter Pan and had it brought into the park at night so that the children seeing it the next day would think the fairies had brought it.

One warm August afternoon I strolled through the gardens in London and suddenly came upon this statue of Peter Pan. It was on a stump-like foundation, and the figure in a dresslike garment was holding a flute. The right hand of the little figure was bent above the shoulder and so lifelike had Frampton made it that I could almost see the child jumping down from the perch and running through the grass to play with the children.

Barrie loved children, and he gave all his profits from writing to charity, helping many of the poor children of London. As he watched the children at play in the park, their make-believe games, their faith in fairies and everlasting happiness, he wished that adults might recapture some of the joys of childhood.

The children saw the fairy rings where the "little people"

came out and danced in the gardens at night. The little creatures did good deeds for the poor. So real were the little people that Barrie wrote his immortal story about Peter Pan.

Somewhere along life's way the fairy world ends. Does it really have to end? When I walk out in the early morning of spring and see the cardinal on a branch, look down at the early English primroses blooming along the garden path, lift my eyes to the rhododendrons along the border, feel the soft morning breeze against my face, smell the aroma of cooking bacon from some kitchen, hear the song of the thrush from the haw tree, then I become young and alive and aware of the wonderful, wonderful world I live in. It is a new day as though I had never walked down the lane before.

If you have lost the spirit of Peter Pan, reach out and regain it. Each day God calls to us to rise up and live and be happy. We do not need to grow old in spirit. Can't you hear the words, "Somewhere I hear my Savior calling, follow me, follow me, follow me"?

Some people do not understand what Jesus meant when he said we must become as little children to enter the kingdom. All he means is that we renew our joy and our hopes and our vision with each new day, that through this new day we can walk with the joy and enthusiasm of a child.

He Was Just a Taxi Driver

"O let the nations be glad and sing for joy: for
thou shalt judge the people righteously, and gov-
ern the nations upon earth."
                                        Psalm 67:4

How long has it been since you have sung the words of
"God Bless America"? It was not until I met a taxi driver
in Holland in 1947, that the words to the song really had
meaning to me.

America is so big and so wonderful with its blending of
many nations. America is people, people with hearts that care
and love. Whenever there is need in the world American
planes rush in food and medical supplies and clothing. It is
not by accident that our country has already celebrated its
bicentennial year. The ability to survive as a democracy for
two hundred years while many of the world's people have
gone through revolution, dictatorship, poverty, and loss of
civil rights can be attributed to religion that has guided our
governments and our people.

If we were to take the teachings of Jesus out of our country,
our bookshelves would be half-empty, our law books filled
with blank pages, our art galleries with barren walls.

A short time after the Second World War, I went to the
Netherlands to visit Raoul Oberman who lived along Malie-
baan in Utrecht. When he was a boy of fourteen, he was
loaded on a train going to Germany to become a slave laborer
in a German munitions plant. With all the cunning of a
boy, he managed to escape from the train before it reached
the German border.

I met Raoul in school in England, and he invited me to
visit his home at the end of the school. At Utrecht I engaged

a taxi and went bouncing over paving stones, up over canals, and down narrow streets. Finally the taxi driver pulled up before a four-story house.

I held out a five-dollar bill. "I am sorry I have nothing smaller. I just arrived in Holland this morning and I have not had time to get Dutch money." The driver shook his head, and I was surprised that five dollars was not enough.

"It isn't that," he said. "You don't owe me anything." He saw the puzzled look in my face. "You are an American, aren't you? I was a schoolteacher when the war broke out. I was put into a factory to work. I had three small children. Our cows were shipped to Germany. Many of our people starved. We could not have survived had it not been for the food packages shipped to us from America. My children had powdered milk two or three times a week. I don't think there is a Dutch family that did not receive food packages from America. Now, do you understand why I cannot take your money?" He wiped his eyes. "You Americans saved so many lives. My wife and I often said we hoped that someday we could do something for you."

I couldn't see clearly either for my tears. But in my heart came the words of "God Bless America," words that would forever have a special meaning to me. My country!

He Will Walk Again

"Teach me thy way, O Lord; I will walk in thy truth."

Psalm 86:11

I remember the summer of 1950. Polio was so bad that summer that children were not permitted to go to a movie or a picnic or swimming or to any other public places. Mothers were terrified at the plague which was so feared because its cause was unknown. Summer was a nightmare and the newspapers printed stories of the crippling disease that seemed to strike children more than adults.

Carl Emerson lived on a side street in Batesville. In early August his youngest son, Freddie, just past his fifth birthday, came down with polio. Freddie survived and went home from the hospital. Doctors were hesitant to say whether he would ever walk again. During the warm August days the boy lay on a blanket in the front yard of his home.

Mrs. Emerson did not say much, but she prayed for a miracle. Freddie's father said again and again, "He will walk again. My son will recover. He will walk." His faith was untouchable.

One afternoon I stopped by to chat with Freddie. He was a beautiful child, with an active and alert mind. It seemed such a waste that the boy might never walk again. But while I was there the boy's father came home. He pulled a small teddy bear out of his pocket and dropped it on the grass about a foot from the boy's hands. I reached to pick up the toy and lay it in the boy's lap.

"Leave it there," Mr. Emerson said.

I put it back. Freddie made an attempt to reach the toy and when he couldn't he cried. It seemed cruel to me. The father brought home toys on other days. Always he did the same thing—placed the toy beyond the reach of the boys hands. I was gone then for over a month to New York. When I came back, I brought a gift for Freddie, a woolly toy horse.

Freddie was out on his blanket as usual and his mother was sitting in a chair nearby knitting. She greeted me and seeing the present for Freddie said: "Don't give it to him. May I have it?"

She dropped the toy three feet from Freddie. He rolled over on his stomach and slowly he dug his knees and elbows into the ground, inching closer and closer to the toy horse until he could reach out and pick it up.

"He can crawl now," Mrs. Emerson said. "The doctor says he has every chance of regaining full use of his legs and arms. He calls it a miracle. But I call it faith—faith that my husband has in God and in God telling him what to do. Freddie's father never let go of his faith that our son would walk again."

There is much we do not understand. Jesus Christ had much to say about following him. It is a miracle that man can move at all, that he can speak and hear and understand. It is a fearful thing when a doctor says, "I have done all I can." And then God steps into the picture and healing takes place. Carl Emerson believed his faith was a part of the miracle.

Open the Door to Joy

"Behold, I stand at the door, and knock: if any
man hear my voice, and open the door, I will
come in to him."

Revelation 3:20

When you build a wall around yourself and say, "I will
never be hurt again," you may be saying a half-truth. We
think of a wall as a barrier that seals us off from people.
This is not always true.

A wall can separate us from the people who hurt us. Once
separated from these people, we can easily change any inclina-
tion to hate, to that of pity. In the name of Jesus Christ
we ought to have compassion upon any person who has so
little in life that he must tear down by gossip, the people
who strive to do.

The truth many have discovered is that on our side of
the wall we find other people. We are not alone. We say
good-bye to the old and can reach out to new friends and a
new life.

Gloria King challenged the statement that to build a wall
around us means the end of living. "I realized early in life
that I wasn't pretty like the other girls. I tried to overcome
my looks by being nice to people, doing things for them.
My deepest hurt came when I was thirty-two. I had been a
teacher in Madison for ten years. I had a chance to go closer
to home to Bloomington to teach, and I took the job. I thought
when I left Madison there would be a party for me at school.
I expected parents to write notes and thank me for teaching
their children. I thought pupils would come and talk to me
and beg me not to go.

"I had coached plays without pay, taken tickets at basketball games, sponsored classes. On the last day of school as I packed my books and personal things in boxes, I expected the principal to come down to my room and thank me for teaching and wish me luck. But I walked out of the building that evening with the depressed feeling that nobody cared.

"I was surprised when I moved back to Bloomington at the change in the town. There were new people, strangers to me. Many of my old friends were no longer there. I planned to start a new life. I would simply walk away from the people who didn't want to be friends. And all at once I found myself to be a happy person once I stopped trying to please others. I found that there were wonderful people all around me. They were genuine, friendly, reaching out. It was a new experience."

Gloria King had learned that looking back can sometimes be enslaving. She learned that there are always new doors in life to step through. Always new friends to make. God is forever saying to us that life is a challenge, that we go forward.

When you awaken tomorrow, make yourself a promise that you will cultivate three new friends. Unless we go on making new friends, we soon find ourselves without friends. Jesus Christ in many of his teachings encouraged people to look up and walk into new lives.

You Are Greater Than You Think

"I was dumb with silence, I held my peace, even
from good; and my sorrow was stirred."
Psalm 39:2

How long has it been since you stopped to think about
the good qualities in your life that cause people to love you?
My mother used to say, "They are the little people of the
world." She was talking about people who seemed to spend
a great deal of time talking about people, running them down,
telling untruths. As we children grew older we learned the
lesson well that the "gossip" is a person unsuccessful in life,
hoping to pull others to their level.

My mother taught us to always find something to praise
other people for. She said, "Everyone has some good quality."
She was right. She had pity for the gossip. I can remember
her trying to shift the subject when a neighbor came over
with a tale about somebody. She would say, "Alice, you have
such a nice-looking garden." Or, "That was a pretty wash
you had out in your yard Monday."

There wasn't much color to Miss Summers. She never got
married. All she ever did was work at the telephone exchange
through the week and go to church on Sunday. When Stella
Winters said she was giving up the Willing Workers Sunday
School class after eighteen years, the question came up as
to who would take her place. "Miss Summers knows her Bible
from end to end." Someone else said, "Her? She is a mouse.
She couldn't teach a class." Another comment, "We need
somebody with some pep and who will be a worker."

Faye Wilson was asked to teach, but she wasn't regular.
Her family had a boat and went to the lake about every other

Sunday. One Sunday Miss Summers was asked to substitute when no one else was willing to teach. In her shy way Miss Summers said, "I will."

Miss Summers was late to class the next Sunday because she had been arranging the altar flowers for church. There was no one at the teacher's table. Thelma Woods spoke up, "Miss Summers, the class has taken a vote and we all want you to be our teacher."

At the end of six months with shy, little Miss Summers as teacher the class has grown from seventeen to over forty young married people. Miss Summers was soft-spoken, but she had a way of making people feel important. She was always saying in class, "That was a good answer." Or, "What do you think?" She pushed them into meaningful jobs in the church in a way that made class members feel it was their idea. She brought out the best in people.

Miss Summers seemed to know about the heartaches, the dreams, the struggles of people. She made them feel successful. She asked questions that everyone could answer whether they had read the lesson or not. "I want everyone in the class to say something before the bell rings," she would say. Before, two or three had done all the talking. One day she said, "I know how important it is to be recognized and to be appreciated. You see I used to be the shy one in class."

These Are the People I Love

"I am the bread of life: he that cometh to me
shall never hunger; and he that believeth in me
shall never thirst."
John 6:35

"I work with the people I love," Anna Reeves said to the
newspaper reporter who came to her schoolroom one afternoon. "When I graduated from a two-year teacher college,
I thought a wonderful new life lay before me. I had my heart
set on getting a job as an English teacher in my home high
school. I cried when the trustee told me there was no opening."

"I'm sorry, Anna. I just filled the job yesterday. I know
you will be a good teacher. Tell you what you do. I talked
to Al Lundy yesterday—trustee over in Benton Township.
He has an opening for a teacher in District seven. Might
not be too bad with a dozen or twenty kids and seven miles
from your house."

Miss Reeves took the job. The pay was eight hundred dollars
a year with ten dollars a month for janitor work which she
agreed to do. When Miss Reeves unlocked the school door
two days before the opening of school and walked into the
school room she felt sick at heart. It was a dingy room with
torn blinds, black oiled floor, fifteen or twenty carved up desks
of various sizes, a cupboard holding a hundred worn books,
a faded globe, and a phonograph on a stand by a well-worn
teacher's desk. The chalkboard was chipped and the walls
of the room were painted a dark green with cobwebs filling
the corners all the way up to the high ceiling.

Miss Reeves wept. She had come from college with modern
classrooms and equipment, fresh from the halls of great teachers and bright students. She felt a terrible loneliness as the

country kids began arriving the first day of school, barefooted, in old, but well-washed overalls, faded but well-pressed dresses. She was soon to learn that most parents never had gone beyond the eighth grade. One of the boys told her the first day that two teachers had been "run out" in the past five years.

Miss Reeves applied the Scriptures to her teaching, believing that the kids were coming for some of that bread of life, that it was her duty to teach them in subjects, manners, and compassion. April came and a week before school ended the trustee walked into the schoolroom one afternoon just at dismissal time.

"Miss Reeves," he began. "We hear you have applied for a job at Monroe over in Ohio. We don't want you to go. I can give you nine hundred dollars."

The children sat quietly in their seats, and there was a commotion at the door as parents came into the room and stood along the back wall. Miss Reeves looked into their faces. She saw the farmers who had left their work in the fields to be there. She looked around the room. There were new blinds and lace curtains at the windows which the mothers had made. The floor was bright yellow with thick varnish, the walls of the schoolroom a soft yellow. The farmers had come on Saturdays during the cold winter and worked hours sanding the black oil out of the floor and painting the walls. There was a new teacher's desk at the front of the room and new books in the shelves.

"We love you because of what you've done for our kids," a mother said.

I Wear a Mask and No One Knows

"Honour thy father and thy mother: that thy
days may be long upon the land which the Lord
thy God giveth thee."
Exodus 20:12

If you watch a program on television about juvenile court, you will try to decide each case before the judge does. Sometimes you will say, "I don't know what he can do."

Almost always the conflict is between child and adult, not between child and the world. A child struggles to be free of restraints. Parents separated by a generation just can't seem to reach their children. Parents say, "Our children see no wrong in drinking, using drugs, speeding in cars, staying out all night, skipping school, defying us in what we want them to do."

A wise parent, Mrs. DeLane thinks differently. "I think many children *do* see wrong; the wrong they do is in rebellion against a world they cannot accept. Esther Feins is a good lesson for us. She was in the freshman class at Moore's High School. She could go to a movie with the girls after school and go home when she wanted to. Her girlfriends envied her because they had to call home after school, get permission to go someplace after school, and say what time they would be home. My daughter, Lou Anne, said to Esther one day how lucky she must feel to be free to do what she wanted to do."

"You think I'm lucky," Esther replied? "I wish my mother cared enough about me to want to know where I am after school. I don't think she cares if I ever come home."

A few days ago I was visiting in the home of a member of the church when a teenage boy started out the front door.

His mother asked him where he was going and when he would be home. This was his reply, "I don't have to tell you where I am going or when I will be home." He slammed the door and was gone.

The hurt in the boy's mother's eyes made me want to go and get the boy and shake the "daylights" out of him. I could see her mind working as she wondered where she failed him. And I wondered too. Who built the barrier? Suppose the boy had walked over and put his arm around his mother, kissed her on the cheek, and told her where he was going and when he would be home? What has happened to love?

You will always find both boys and girls hanging around the desk of Orville Wooters, a local high school teacher. He talks to them about their dogs, their jobs, their old cars, their vacation trips. He kids them about their hair, the patches on their blue jeans. He talks to them about dating and about jobs and listens to them. Once I heard him say, "You never find me sitting behind the teacher's desk—that symbol of authority."

And he added, "They surprise me many times by taking off their masks and sharing with me weeping hearts, conflicts that nearly smother them, dreams, and hopes. I feel humble to have learned the secret of caring about kids and listening to them. Maybe if more parents had time to listen, the juvenile courts would not be so busy."

Walk Gently Past My Grave

"Whosoever liveth and believeth in me shall never die."

John 11:26

It was a wonderful night for Halloween. The church basement rang with the laughter of girls and boys dressed in animal, fairy, and hobo costumes, playing games and doing stunts. Iva Linginfelter was in the midst of the fun. Iva was sixty-seven years old. She had spent most of her life helping children to have a happy life.

The next morning she slipped away into a world where youth is eternal. There was a memorial service for her one quiet Sunday afternoon. There were flowers like she had loved in her lifetime and people for whom she had opened the windows of the world. They quietly slipped into pews and sat remembering her, as organ music filled the house of God.

I walked into that church this late June afternoon, walked past the tall stained glass window and paused to read the small bronze plate, "In Loving Memory of Iva Linginfelter." And it seemed to me that I could hear the voices of children ringing through the empty church.

"I will always remember her, young in heart, teaching a children's class for so many years," Phyllis Foreman said. "I remember how her home was always open to the children of the neighborhood and the bottomless cookie jar, and her soft laughter."

"I wish I could be remembered like her," said Freda Reynolds. "When I die I want my ashes scattered to the four winds of the world. I want to be remembered as I am now. I don't want anyone to come and see me in a nursing home.

When I can no longer comb my hair and put on my makeup, I want to quietly withdraw from life as Iva Linginfelter did. How God must have loved her to open the door to his kingdom to her in her hour of joy."

What Jesus said has been cherished by men for over two thousand years. The spirit of man lives into eternity upon this earth. Who will ever forget Edison who lighted the world? Who can forget Bell and the magic telephone he gave us? Who can forget a mother who held us? Who can forget people who have touched us?

Once Iva Linginfelter said: "I am happy because I know that I do not walk alone through life. His Spirit walks always beside me. I will not always be bound to this earth. Life seems so beautiful ahead, to be free to walk in spirit over the hills of my childhood will be heaven to me. To watch over the ones I love, and to be in God's living presence forever, makes me feel so warm and happy inside."

I said this prayer when I walked past the window given in memory of Iva Linginfelter: "Help us, God, to usher in a new world of kindness and love. Keep the dream in our heart of the time when we, too, shall walk in spirit over the earth. The seed must die to give life to the new plant and so it is with man. It is in dying that we live again. When I am gone walk gently past my grave. But do not think that I am dead. Only that I walk in a new world of joy and beauty."

Paul Hamilton Day

"Let your light so shine before men, that they
may see your good works."
Matthew 5:16

I first saw Paul Hamilton pushing a broom, sweeping up
loose gravel and trash in front of Jody's restaurant. I thought
how useful his work must be, helping to keep the town beautiful. Then I learned that he was in charge of the streets and
took his turn sweeping when needed.

I last saw him stand before an audience of over two hundred
of his friends at a recognition dinner. There were tears in
his eyes as he tried to express his thanks for the dinner given
in appreciation of him, thanks to the people of the little town
of a thousand people who had come to honor him as their
friend and as a great artist.

Paul Hamilton always used his hands, whether pushing a
broom to help keep his town beautiful or holding a brush
to create paintings of lasting beauty. He grew up in Richmond,
Indiana, attending the elementary schools, playing up and
down the banks of the Whitewater River where he saw the
crumbling foundations of old woolen mills and bridges. As a
growing boy he was always busy, washing windows, raking
leaves, running errands, delivering papers for spending money
and school books.

Before he finished high school he got a job at the Hoosier
Store, carrying out trash and sweeping floors and clerking.
Then one day his chance came—a chance to use his artistic
talents. He was assigned to assist in window decorating. His
boss was so impressed that he promoted Paul to chief decorator
and paid for an art course in Morton High School, the only

formal training that the artist ever had.

Paul Hamilton moved to Centerville, a historic town on the old Cumberland Trail. There he was employed for many years. He drew maps of water lines, spotted hydrants and sewers. But when his work for the city was over, he hurried home to pick up his brush. His love for history led him to specialize in old mills, toll houses, bridges, buildings of great historic interest to a nation approaching a bicentennial.

Paul's pictures went to art exhibits and were sold and found their way into homes all over the country. He went into the elementary schools and freely gave his time teaching art classes on how to sketch, where to find material, and teaching appreciation of the country to the children.

He was in the midst of painting the old Salisbury Court-house, said to be the oldest standing log courthouse in the old Northwest Territory, when a knock came at his studio door. How surprised he was when he was told that "Paul Hamilton Day" would be the climax to American Education Week—that he would be honored by the community in the bicentennial year.

Former employers, friends from distant cities, and towns-people crowded into the dining room to honor Paul Hamilton. They came from all walks of life to honor a humble man who had never sought honor. "I thought an artist had to be dead before anyone remembered him," said a childhood friend of Paul's who drove seventy-five miles to attend the dinner. "This is the biggest event in Centerville's history, honoring a great man who is living."

I Have Heard You Cry

"Am I my brother's keeper?"
Genesis 4:9

Down every side street in every town is a man who has helped a boy go to summer camp. There are mothers who have guided boys and girls into happiness. The beauty and compassion of God flows forever through the channel of man's heart.

Elizabeth Gurney Fry, mother of twelve children, found the time to help us have a better world. She spoke out in a day when women were oppressed, not only for women's rights but also for better treatment of the poor and the imprisoned.

She was born under the shadow of the great Cathedral of Norwich. She took wretched children from the streets on tours of the cathedral. She showed them the mortar between the stones, the work of her grandfather who had helped to build the cathedral.

She saw the rich in jewels and fine clothes who came into the cathedral to pray, careful not to brush against the beggers. The clanking of chains in the streets was ever in her ears, the sound of fetters riveted to the legs of men breaking stone in the cold drizzle of the winter. And on days without end Elizabeth Fry witnessed the children and women, who were thrown into prison cells with men. They pleaded for food from the bars of their unheated prison. All of them—young girls, hardened criminals, prostitutes, maids accused of stealing as little as a thimble, girls who had run away from brutal fathers, thieves and murderers—pleaded for scraps of food from people passing by. Armed guards were always present, free to be in any part of the prison with no privacy for the women. Three hundred offenses were punishable by death, among them shoplifting.

Elizabeth Fry, using her influence, got permission from the governor to enter the prison. She led the people in prayer. She started a school for the children. She brought cloth from her husband's store and taught the women to make clothes. She asked other women to help her and was successful in getting separate quarters in the prison for the women. Mats to sleep on and blankets for cover were brought into the prison for the first time.

Elizabeth Fry became famous. Her love and desire to help the unfortunate took her to prisons all over England. She was invited by the French and Belgium governments to visit their prisons and asylums and to help them bring reform. Holland and Germany asked for help, and Elizabeth Fry was received by kings and queens and prime ministers. She believed prisons should be operated for reformation and not for revenge.

"If you build dark, unlighted, unfurnished cells, the day may come when your children will occupy them," she said. She had a dream, and she gave her life to make it come true and earned the name "Friend of Humanity."

So many people follow in her footsteps today. The United Nations is one example of the greatest dream of mankind, to understand and bring peace and prosperity to the child in darkest Africa, as well as to the slums of New York City. God does not allow man to live in peace as long as there is injustice and need for changing the conditions under which man lives.

Her Name Will Be Remembered

"Lord, remember me when thou comest into thy
kingdom."
Luke 23:42

The name of Imogene Voss will not be forgotten. She lived
in poverty all her life, and she lived alone in a small tumbled-
down house on a side street of her town. The only thing
she owned of value was her love for her hometown.

All who enter the City Building of Centerville will see
her name on a large bronze plaque in the entrance hall, an
expensive plaque given in memory of the men who served
in the wars to preserve democracy.

Imogene Voss scrubbed floors for fifty years in office buildings, washed woodwork, cleaned restrooms, emptied ash trays,
washed windows, and scrubbed steps. She was seventy years
of age when she got up from her knees for the last time
and put her scrub brush away. She was tired.

But when she retired there was a luxury hardtop waiting
to pick her up and take her in the parade on Memorial Day
to the services in the cemetery. She was so proud to ride
behind the band and the marching scouts and veterans.

I can still see her coming into church on a Memorial morning. The last three years of her life she was assisted by a
veteran who helped her to a seat. She always sat with them
as they visited a different church each Memorial day.

I remember seeing her for the first time over fifty years
ago waiting in the small ticket office of the interurban bus
line for the seven o'clock car that would take her to Richmond
where she worked. She was a frail woman, short in height,
and weighed about one hundred and five pounds. Often when

she came home from work, she would babysit.

Soon after Imogene Voss died a bulldozer moved in and leveled her little house. She was forgotten for a time. And then the bank released to the newspaper that she had left thousands of dollars in bequests to the churches and cemeteries of her town. Her will was carried out with one exception. Perhaps from her home in heaven she will look down and forgive her townspeople who insisted that her name be engraved on the tablet she gave in memory of those who served their country in time of war.

She went quietly without fanfare to meet her Maker, finding a lasting peace but leaving behind something to teach us all. A humble life can be great and love is the greatest of all.

Who can judge the thief upon the cross? Jesus saw a broken heart. If he had not forgiven, there would be no forgiveness for any one of us. Like the thief upon the cross, Imogene Voss was a person of humility. Her bequests to the churches will reach to the Middle East with soup and powdered milk for orphan children; her gift to the hospital will be spent for furniture for the children's ward. So much was left to enrich the world from the slender savings week by week by the woman who scrubbed floors to greatness.

The Family Next Door

"Thou shalt love the Lord thy God with all thy
heart, and with all thy soul, and with all thy
strength, and with all thy mind; and thy neighbor
as thyself. And who is my neighbor?"
Luke 10:27, 29

How far away does one need to go to reach out? Sometimes
we look through an alumni magazine and see names of class-
mates or people we have known who have become noted
doctors, reached high positions in industry, or become college
professors, eminent lawyers, great scientists. And we compare
our gift to the world with those who have gone to the top.
Sometimes we feel sad because we dreamed of greatness too.

You are greater than you think. You may always live down
a shady street in a small town. You may never make the
headlines. It wasn't meant that you should. Somewhere out
there in the world may be your son or your daughter—your
gift to the world.

George Reed knew the greatness of his neighbor. He lived
in a white frame house behind a picket fence. When he was
eighty years old, a family of five children moved in next door.

George tended his garden, a garden that got smaller and
smaller each year. One afternoon someone spoke to him.
George looked up from hoeing his garden. A woman was
standing by the fence looking over into his garden. "It is so
hot today. I thought you needed to rest. I've brought you a
glass of lemonade and some cookies right out of the oven."
She smiled, as she reached across the fence. "And please let
me send Bruce over to mow your grass. He doesn't have to
go on his paper route for two hours."

From his hospital bed two weeks later George Reed said
to his nurse, "I have nothing to worry about while I am here.

My neighbors are taking care of my place for me."

And it was true. One of the boys fed George's dog. The family came to visit him every day at the hospital. When George went home from the hospital, a former nurse came over and gave him a shot every morning. When he grew weaker, she carried over his meals, gave him his bath, and then one night George died quietly in his sleep. His one dread was of going to a nursing home. Thanks to his neighbor, he was loved and cared for as though he were a member of the family.

"We are going to miss him now that he is gone," the woman next door said. "It is strange not to see him going out to his garden early in the morning to hoe. I will always see him down on his knees there. I think he prayed over his plants. I never bake cookies but what I think of him. Maybe he thought my family did a lot for him, but he did more for us. My boys learned to give without receiving money from an old man who needed their strong hands and backs. I remember the kind and pleased look in his face when I put my arm around him and helped him to sit up in bed. He gave me something too. I have a rich memory, a richer life. I will always be able to look up and be proud that God asked me and my family to share our love with an old man who needed us."

It Is Not Always Easy to Choose

"Mary hath chosen that good part, which shall
not be taken away from her."
Luke 10:42

Sometimes God asks us to travel a road that is not always
easy. We yearn for adulthood; we hold on to childhood. God
knows what he wants us to do. And he knows that it hurts
to give up that which we love today for the goal of tomorrow.

Elmer Robbins and Thelma Tolsen started going together
when they were freshmen in high school. It was sort of understood that when high school was over they would get married.
Elmer would join his father as a partner in his hardware store.
He would buy a house, marry Thelma, and live happily ever
after, still going to the church of their childhood, seeing old
friends, content and comfortable.

During his senior year Elmer was offered an attractive scholarship to an engineering school in the East, thanks to his
physics teacher who worked to get a scholarship for the boy.
Elmer knew what he wanted. He worked Saturdays and vaca-
tions in the hardware store, and he hated it. He wanted a
job out of doors, a job with adventure, and as a mining engineer
he might go to South America or Africa. It was a challenge.

The scholarship was also a problem. He had to make a
choice, a choice of staying home with security, comfort, the
girl he loved, or going on for five or six years of hard study.
Elmer knew how his father felt, wanting to leave a successful
business to him, the only son. And Elmer weakened one Sunday evening when he walked Thelma to her door after a band
concert in the park. But her final words made him decide
to go to college.

"If you go away to school, Elmer, it is over with us. I can't stand to be separated from you. I love you, Elmer. I want to marry you. I don't want to leave this town and my family. It isn't fair for you to ask me to."

Elmer came home for Christmas, but things had changed. He wanted to go to summer school, and Thelma's letter early in May decided that. "I have to write this letter to you before someone else tells you. I told you I couldn't wait four years for you. You chose college instead of me. I am engaged to be married in August. He is a nice young man and we won't be moving out of Circleville, leaving our families."

Elmer Robbins slowly lighted a match to the letter and watched the flame curl the paper into black ashes. He felt sick inside, but he had three years or more of college before him, and he went immediately and signed up for summer school. His childhood romance was buried forever.

The place you live, the choice of your vocation, the friends you make, have a great bearing on happiness and success. God shows us the way. Sometimes we do not understand why God wants us to do the service he asks us to do. Of course Mary knew the need of cooking and setting the table and placing an ample meal before guests. But when Jesus came she made her choice, to sit at his feet and to talk to him. She chose the good part that could not be taken away from her.

A Place to Climb

How sad are the words: "There is nothing to do. There is no place to go." Many people have adopted the faith of "eat, drink, and be merry, for tomorrow we die."

In recent times the art of looking up has been lost by so many who have forgotten, if they ever knew, the rewarding life of having a dream. The cost is too high, the time is too long, to reach for a dream.

Hanging on the wall in the long hall of the House of Lords in London is a picture of a family in a boat rowing out to a small ship to go to America. They are leaving behind parents, home, and their native land, giving up everything in the hope of finding a new home, a new country, a new life. It is a sad picture because it is not easy to cut ourselves off from all we have ever loved.

A little girl by the name of Pollyanna had a dream. Her dream was to bring happiness into the lives of people who had forgotten how to smile. It became almost a religion with Pollyanna to push people into being happy.

Few contemporary works of fiction have any lasting value. The book clubs greedily grab them up, books that one couldn't have in a church library, let alone in a family room for children to see. Broadway plays appeal to the most base emotions of men. The popular song has become one line repeated in a monotonous refrain. Newspapers have become tools of muckraking. For many rules of morality have been thrown to the winds. Responsible parenthood often has been turned over to social organizations. These have been sad years.

War has had a brutal aftermath on human lives. Drugs for escape. Lawlessness if one doesn't like the rules. Killers in cars on the highways, killers with the right to drink.

And suddenly, lives are empty. There is no home to go back to. There is nothing. Without a place to climb, man is nothing. Perhaps even now there is a turn, to look again at what were once values in life.

Life had little value in the day of Jesus. Then, as now, men yearned for the better life. Jesus believed that dreams could live in the human heart once men learned to have faith in themselves. The lepers, the crippled, the blind, found that faith was the beginning of a new life. Jesus opened doors for them and they lived again.

Sometimes out of great loss, defeat, and heartache it is difficult to lift our eyes again. But we must recover this art of looking up. If we cannot, then all else in life is worthless.

"I sat on the swing on my porch late one afternoon," Bill Bronson said. "I had been fishing all morning. I had played a round of golf in the afternoon. I was home with nothing to do. But what struck me with force was that I wasn't doing anything worthwhile in life. The ringing of the telephone changed my life. Would I serve on the board of directors of the Boys' Club and maybe take some leadership. And I knew at that moment that I had a place to climb."

This Was His Garden

"One thing have I desired of the Lord, that will
I seek after; that I may dwell in the house of
the Lord all the days of my life, to behold the
beauty of the Lord."

Psalm 27:4

I remember when this was his garden. The paths were neatly trimmed and in the spring there were long borders of hyacinths and daffodils and tulips. I can still smell the sweet, deep fragrance of the white and pink and purple hyacinths.

The paths are deep with grass where once he walked. Overhead and free from the weeds and grass the white dogwood and the purple lilacs bloom. The garden gate sags on its hinges and the round lily pool is overgrown with wild raspberries and elder bushes. No matter which way I look I keep hearing the lament of the once proud garden—"I am not loved anymore."

I thank God that I have learned a great lesson today. You have given to your children of the earth a responsibility in life. When his fingers tended the soil and he loved the tender plants, the earth brought forth beauty. Now that he is gone, the earth returns to the way it was.

You send a child into the world, a child created from two cells so small the human eye cannot see them, and you say to man, "I gave you the miracle of the child—now you go on from here." And so we shape the child, we guide him, we laugh and cry over him, and we see him grow into an intelligent human being.

You gave us the earth. You gave man dominion over the earth. If we waste it, we are to blame. If we poison our oceans, we are to blame. If we destroy our soil, we are to blame. If we wage war, we are to blame. You gave us the right to make our choices. I am grateful that the garden taught me how important man is to God.

The hands that cultivated the garden sought after you, God. He never dropped a seed into the earth or planted a bulb but what he prayed a silent prayer that the tiny seed or bulb would burst into a brightly colored flower or a vegetable wholesome to eat.

He said to me once, "Dwell in the house of the Lord all the days of my life? I am dwelling there now. I am living in a state of eternal life. God loves me. Here is his beauty, here among the flowers that I love."

And he stooped and put his knees upon the warm soft soil and carefully pulled a tiny weed from around a white blossom. "God recognized there were weeds in the world. He talks about them in the farmer's field. There will still be plenty when I have freed my garden of them. They keep growing. They will be back. I admire them, the struggle they make to keep living. But my flowers—they seem so tender, so in need of my care."

Somewhere he is in God's garden of eternity. I think as I leave behind me the sagging garden gate that it was here so many times that he walked in his garden and talked to you, God.

She Wore a Yellow Ribbon

"Your heart shall rejoice, and your joy no man
taketh from you."
John 16:22

"She can see your smile. That is what counts." And the woman added, "My mother is ninety-four years old. She doesn't hear."

I was on the seventh floor of Reid Memorial Hospital, making my rounds as a volunteer worker, taking patients in wheel chairs down to physical therapy. "Mrs. Wilson," I said, "I am here to take you to therapy so that you can learn to walk again." Her daughter had combed her gray hair and tied a yellow ribbon on top. To me the yellow ribbon seemed to speak of joy and youth.

Is it really true that a smile is what counts? People in all lands, no matter what language they speak, understand a smile. It says, "I like you. I want to be your friend."

What is it that makes the heart rejoice? What is the joy that no man can take away? It is having in one's heart the knowledge that life is good. The things we use every day have been made by man—the car he drives, the TV set in his family room, the clothes, the airplane, the shoes and hat he wears. None of these was here when the American Indian inhabited the land. Is it reasonable to believe that someone made the stars, the moon, the clouds, the life that is in every plant and animal?

The wind blows, but we do not see it, where it comes from or where it goes. We recognize a friend we have not seen in many years. We recall the places we have traveled.

All of these are real and bring back pleasant times and pleasant places.

The joy that no man can take away is a joy that comes from having faith in oneself as a person. The Gospel of John tells us that a rejoicing heart is essential if one is to live and to dwell in courage and in hope. Joy comes from within and because it does, no man can take it away. People have said, "I am going to find happiness in life." They say this only to find that happiness begins in the human heart. It is not something that you pick up in a new dress or a new automobile.

Happiness can come in the form of a service. Older people sometimes find themselves unneeded in the world. Life takes on meaning for them when their children continue to ask their advice about buying a new home or going into business or buying a new car.

Happiness comes in writing a check for a boy's club or in sending a girl to summer camp or in helping a student through college. Sometimes it is very easy to read in the eyes and on the lips of a person their true feelings. There is so much that can be seen in a smile.

A smile says, "I like you." A smile says, "I am happy today." A smile from another person puts us at ease and we are no longer afraid.

In the movie *The Ten Commandments* Moses, upon seeing his real mother, loved her. But he said to the woman who had reared him as her child, "Yours was the first face I saw leaning over my cradle. I will always love you."

These Are the Books He Loved

"Give me now wisdom and knowledge."
2 Chronicles 1:10

"These are the books he loved. He loved the feel of leather in his hand, but he loved even more the wisdom he found in his books." And she added with pride in her voice, "He stood for all that was fine in life—honesty and dignity, generosity and love."

I stood in the center of the long library of William Dudley Foulke. The spacious rambling home of brick and stone stood on Linden Hill that overlooked the city of Richmond, Indiana. It was soon to feel the march of the bulldozer that would level the landmark of the city's most illustrious citizen. Every trace that he had lived would be forever erased. It was too much to hope that the home of the author and diplomat would be preserved as a museum.

"This was one of his most loved books," she said, as she handed me a black leather bound book of the works of Browning. "He purchased it while on a trip to Italy."

I selected six books from the library of the man who had been my friend. Then she told me that the best of his books would go to the Earlham College Library for a special room, and the busts of Mr. and Mrs. Foulke would be placed as a permanent exhibit of the Richmond Art Association. And I knew that somebody cared, something of his life would be left for the next generation to see.

As I walked slowly down the path from Linden Hill, I stopped to take one last look at the mansion. The house was filled with so many memories. William Dudley Foulke was the author of several books. He had been a successful attorney, a connoisseur of the fine arts, a man of great faith in God. He had been a friend of presidents, an untiring worker in the establishment of Civil Service for federal employees.

One day he said to me as I sat with him in his library, "I find that the truly great people of the world are those who have changed the world for better, and they have been men of deep religious faith."

Yes, it is through faith that men have unlocked the secrets of God's world. Few men ever gave it a thought as they walked across the sands of the ocean that the sands could be changed to glass. But a man did dream. And because of this man's wisdom we can take an inexpensive raw material and make glass stronger than steel, more fragile than paper. Take it away and the microscope and the light bulb are gone.

The most profound discoveries have come through man's faith, wisdom, and desire to improve life. William Dudley Foulke loved books because they contained the knowledge of what men had learned, and in addition, men's highest thoughts in poetry and inspiration. He believed that through love for his fellowmen there came purpose and fulfillment in life.

It is sad to walk down South Eighteenth Street today where Foulke once lived, but in a sense this gifted man still walks across the green lawn, his spirit alive in the trees, in the winds, and in my heart.

Born to Be Great

He was born on the north side of the tracks, but he became one of the first citizens of his hometown. Few boys went to high school in his day. Large families and low wages caused many a boy to drop out of school and work to help support the family. Only the children of the shopkeepers and the professional clan went to high school. But Robert Blue had a dream.

He had to overcome many obstacles to reach the night when he walked across the stage to get a coveted diploma. During his years in school, he sought jobs all over town to earn money to buy school clothes, to pay for school supplies, and to help his family. There were many discouraging days when he didn't have the money to go to all the basketball games and attend other school activities.

His first full-time job when he got out of school was with the United States Army. For a time the world forgot him. Then, a few people noticed a boy sweeping the floors and the front steps of the hometown bank. Time went by and he was named manager of the bank in his hometown. Robert Blue had proven once again that a boy could rise to the top in America. But he wanted more.

He ran for City Council. He became president of the council, a job equal to being mayor in a city. He kept walking forward. As a member of the Lions Club he accompanied a truck loaded with clothing to the territories of the Indians in the Southwest. On the trip he learned a great deal about his country. He saw yellow school buses carrying Indian children to modern elementary and high schools. He loved the beauty of the Southwest.

When Robert Blue returned home, he had another dream. He wanted to share the love he had for America. Soon he was showing pictures of his wonderful America, using sound and three slide projectors and three screens. Few could view these pictures and his commentary along with them without tears and a lump in the throat as a new love for one's country was created by the program.

When the community needed a leader to be chairman of the United Fund drive year after year, Robert Blue always said, "I will." He collected and banked funds for the annual children's Christmas party sponsored by the fire department. He gave his time as a Jaycee. He became coordinator with the town and the bicentennial commission to put on a great celebration for the nation's two-hundredth birthday.

He headed up a drive to raise money in his community for the building of Indiana University East. He has not changed much from the boy—shy, quiet, humble, walking the second mile in service to his community, in love for his country. But he became the first citizen of the town because he had a dream.

There Will Be Peace

"Glory to God in the highest, and on earth peace,
good will toward men."

Luke 2:14

There is a tall statue standing west of the rose gardens at the United Nations, a statue showing a sword being beaten into a plowshare. It is a sobering thought that this statue is a gift from the Russian people, a country where religion is not encouraged. But the statue represents the longing of the world to be free from conflict.

A father once said, "I stood here in the street and cheered my boy as he marched behind the band in his uniform and carried a gun. I didn't know I was cheering him on in his death march. When the enemy lost a battle I went to a tavern and drank beer with my friends to celebrate the victory.

"Now I know, because my son died on a foreign battlefield, that the enemy cheered when they won a battle. We fathers of the world celebrated with beer the deaths of the sons of the world. We have been so blind."

Nations have struggled for centuries to build peace through alliances, treaties, and world organizations to slow the march to conflict. Someday success will come. A twenty-three year-old girl, a Chinese guide in the United Nations building was asked this question by a high school senior, "Is the United Nations doing any good?"

Her answer was almost a whisper, "It is the only thing that is holding the world together." She was thinking of the problems of hunger, economics, government in new countries. Men *do* want to be self-governed. Men do want jobs, security, and the right to control what is in their land. So many resources in Africa and other parts of the world are controlled by other countries, by foreign investors. It is humiliating to be a pauper because you cannot have what is within your country.

It takes a lot of love and giving to keep a family together. The United Nations is a family. It is a family that cares about its people. The people of Israel have said, "The greatest gift the United Nations has given to us is to provide schoolrooms for the education of our children." No mention was made of arms and amunition for protection. Nations, like families, have high hopes in their children, and education is the key to freedom and understanding.

It is not easy to slow down the program for more bombs, more airplanes, more missiles, fortified borders, suspicion and distrust; to substitute a program for more schools, seeds, tractors, fertilizers, newspapers, roads, factories, housing, appliances. Not easy, but it will come.

There are so many good things within our reach. Luke states a truth that men seek for, peace on earth and good will toward men. Love must replace distrust. It was sad to stand and look at the watch towers, dogs, and barbed wire on the Austrian-Hungarian border in 1968 and then two weeks later to cross so easily from the United States into Canada. Dreams do come true.

Does Anybody Care?

"By this shall all men know that ye are my disciples, if ye have love one to another."
John 13:35

Lois Harvey tells of her experience one morning on a routine trip to town. "I rode an elevator up fourteen floors. People touched shoulders. There was no talking, no one spoke. I sat in a doctor's office for over one hour. On all sides were sad, sometimes apprehensive people, people with problems and worries. No one spoke to his neighbor. I stood at a grocery checkout counter. No customer ahead of me spoke to the checkout girl, simply handed over their money and picked up their change.

"I came back home depressed because of the unfriendly world in which I lived. Then the thought came to me—friendship begins with me. I resolved that the next time I found myself among strangers I would see them as people like me, in need of companionship, company, and sometimes a need to talk.

"It wasn't easy to understand, this idea of caring about people. I found it the next day when I visited in Reid Memorial Hospital. A woman in a gray uniform of the Red Cross volunteer sat in the emergency waiting room to talk to people there waiting to hear of emergency patients brought in. I talked to a woman in a pink coat, a Reid volunteer who was on the telephone between surgery and relatives to comfort and inform them of operations in progress or recovery-room patients.

"I saw a man in a red coat pushing a patient to physical therapy, heard him talking to the patient and cheering him up. I stepped aside at the elevator to allow a pretty teenage candystriper pass with a bouquet of flowers for a patient. I became aware that the hospital was represented in every department by some volunteer worker who cared.

"The next time I got on an elevator I said hello to the other passenger. I commented on the plant for a patient that the visitor carried. I got a smile and a thank you. Next I held a door open for an elderly man, and I said good morning to him. He smiled and thanked me.

"I said good morning to the clerk at the ribbon counter in the department store. Before, my first words had always been that I wanted something: 'I want to buy a yard of blue ribbon,' or 'I want a pair of black gloves.' But how nice it was when I began to acknowledge the person there to wait on me before demanding to be shown an item of goods.

"And I found that my day became a happier day. In caring about other people I began to care more about myself. I felt I had a place in society. I found that people often needed me and the comfort I gave them when they were hurting deep inside but could not ask for help.

"Yes, I want to be a follower of him who said he would know me by my love for another."

Hope Is a Building Stone

"It is good that a man should both hope and
quietly wait for the salvation of the Lord."
Lamentations 3:26

In the novel *The Masquerader*, written by Katherine Cecil Thurston at the beginning of the century, the character, Chilcote says, "Hopes belong to the past." A brilliant man, Chilcote rises to high position in British Parliament, proof in this case that hope is never a dead thing.

Hope has been a building stone in all ages for growth and achievement. Back in the Sunday School of my childhood we used to sing a song that went like this, "Unanswered yet the prayer your lips have uttered." God's answer to those who wait is revealing so many times. True, he cannot give us back our youth. True, we sometimes cannot understand the reason for death. But many times God asks us to do something to bring to reality that for which we pray.

Every school, every hospital, every library, every child's summer camp was once a dream. Those who dreamed gave their time and their money to make the dream come true. We live in a day when so many people feel it is "his job to do the work that needs to be done." Then we go into another community and find that almost everyone is involved in community activities. "I am sorry that we can't use you at the moment," a would-be volunteer at a state hospital was told. "We have a list of people waiting to give their time here."

Sometimes we feel that a nursing home is a sad place. It may be sad, but it is not without love, love of people who care. A few days ago over thirty youngsters from a fourth-grade elementary school came into the Center Nursing Home.

The children had Valentines they had made for the patients. There were cookies and fruit to be distributed. And then the children sang in each wing. They went into every room with a gift and a bright hello to the patients.

What is hope? A patient said, "I can't wait until another group comes in. They will. Every week there are children, there are musical groups, there are devotional groups, and people from everywhere. Of course we get lonely here, but we have so much to be thankful for because people care about us, people on the outside."

What is hope? Hope is planning to become a greater person day after day. Hope is really looking for someone to help. Hope is faith in man's climb to the kingdom of God. Hope is what makes life still worthwhile even with its pain, its disappointments, its trials, and its work. Hope is knowing that God cares.

Hope is saying early in the morning, "What new friend will I meet today?" It is in the mind because we put it there. But perhaps the brightest jewel we wear in our crown comes from helping another to have hope in life.

I'll Cry Today

"Jesus wept."

John 11:35

I am glad that Jesus wept because of the death of a friend. Even the Jews who were present saw the great sorrow Jesus felt as they said, "Behold how he loved him" (v. 36).

What's wrong with emotions? Why do we hear people say to a boy, "You mustn't cry." Why is it wrong for a man to shed tears but quite proper for a woman to do so?

When we witness a great sacrifice in real life or even on the screen, why may we not weep? I stood on a street in Chicago a few years ago, and saw an apartment building burning. The police had roped off the area, and the fireman were doing all within human power to save lives. Not far from me two police held by force a woman who had twice broken through the lines crying, "My baby, my baby is up there. I left her for a few minutes to go to the grocery. You got to let me through—my baby, my baby!"

And then, a fireman came out of the door of the apartment building carrying a frightened child in his arms. He heard her cries and walked over and laid the small boy in her arms. Then he turned away. She didn't say anything, but the fireman saw the look in her eyes—no words could have told him more. His eyes were tear-streaked too. And I thought of the times when an inferno of a fire prevented firemen from reaching victims in time and how they must shed tears because of the lives they could not save.

Mrs. Barry said: "I am always so glad when my grandchildren come to visit. I just count the very short hours until they leave for home. There is the usual hugging and good-byes and waving until the car is out of sight. Then I go back into my house and cry. I cry because I love them so much. I cry because God has given me so much happiness in my fine grandchildren. I cry because the time is so short when I am with them."

It would be a repetition to say that to really understand happiness one must know sorrow. There has to be a way of measuring our gratitude, our happiness. Ralph Harris once said, "My childhood was such a struggle. I went without many things I really needed. My folks never knew if they would have the rent money or money for my schoolbooks. We made out, but it was a struggle. Now I have plenty and more than I need. But I live a very simple life. I am grateful that I have the things that I need. I am grateful that the struggle is over. Yet, as I look back, I know that having to work is the reason for a man's success. I feel sorry for the boy or girl born rich into the world."

What's wrong with saying, "I like you?" What's wrong with telling a woman you see in a store, "You are the most beautiful woman I have seen today"? What's wrong with saying to a man, "When you get tired of that necktie you are wearing, I'd be glad to have it"?

Why do we hide our feelings and walk through the world like robots? Why do we not tell people how we feel about them?

One Life to Give

There was an old Sunday School song that went like this, "I gave, I gave my life for thee, What hast thou giv'n for me?"

Whenever you feel that your day has been one that you haven't accomplished very much, try listing on a sheet of paper all the good things you have done for people in your lifetime and the wrongs you have committed. You will be surprised at the things you have given away.

A man in a nursing home said to me a few days ago, "I was a florist for over forty years. I can remember the corsage I made for a girl going to her first senior prom. I remember the Saturdays I took flowers to a church for an afternoon wedding. I remember the bouquets I made that went to the hospital. I always felt that I was working with God, helping to bring beauty and joy into the lives of others.

"I imagined the look in the eyes of the teenage girl when he presented the corsage to her. You know—she spent hours on her hair and her clothes and was the prettiest ever in her life. And then the flowers—well that was the frosting on the cake. Flowers always seemed to say, I love you. Yes, I always felt like a boy again when I sent out flowers for a prom or a wedding.

"And then on Mother's Day it was a different kind of a feeling. Mothers mean so many things to so many people. When I stood up on the platform at the small-town school and reached for my high school diploma, I wasn't really think-

"

ing about myself. I was thinking about my mother sitting down there in the fourth row. I was thinking about the lunches she packed for me. I was thinking about her reminding me that it was time to get my hair cut. I was thinking about the clean clothes she always had in my dresser drawer. I was thinking about the things she sometimes went without for me—like the time she sold a calf she had planned to keep so I would have money for my senior trip."

He looked out the window from his wheelchair for a long time. Then he said, "I've always remembered her selling the calf. It was a sacrifice for me because she loved me. I did odd jobs when I could to earn money, but it was not enough for the trip. She wanted me to have what the others had. Her love wasn't enough. It was a happy day in my life when I drove into the lane of our small farm some six years later and presented my mother with two purebred Hereford heifers. It was the beginning of small herd for her."

I thought of the widow who cast in her two mites. She gave them in love, too, because her heart was filled with the spirit of giving.

You Are My Friend

"Have I been so long time with you, and yet
hast thou not known me, Philip?"
John 14:9

If you pause for a moment on a corner on Fifth Street in Covington, Kentucky, you will see embedded in the sidewalk a bronze marker, the gift of school children to a policeman who stood on the corner and helped them safely across on their way to school.

Children who remembered him said, "He was our friend." What a wonderful tribute, to be remembered as a friend. The policeman died before he was forty years of age. I do not know how or why he died. I know he faced death every day in fighting crime, as well as in helping people. To die so young must have left a deep impression on the children when they came to the corner one morning and he was not there.

If you pause for a moment it will not be difficult for you to remember when you helped a child to discover life and when you brought laughter into the lives of others. Often we do not know ourselves. We forget our contribution to the lives of others. As children of God, we have a special reason to love and rejoice. When we lack love for ourselves we become crippled and cannot put forth the best that is in us. Jesus leaves no question about our worth when he says, "Thou shalt love thy neighbor as thyself" in Matthew 19:19.

While some people think that pride is a sin and that man is a vile animal, Jesus Christ did not think so. It is man who has put himself in low esteem. Harold Williams tells the story of a town loafer who died. He had been content to do a few odd jobs while his wife took in washings to support the family. The new minister surprised many who came to the memorial services for the town loafer. Who could say anything good about the man?

"There is hardly a man in this town," Reverend Martin said, "who cannot remember when Duke Bowen whittled him out a whistle from elder."

And that was the story of the town loafer who spent most of his time on a bench with his knife and elder. And his wife privately added, "Duke had a bad heart condition. He couldn't do any kind of physical labor." And the town folks bowed their head a little when they knew, for they had judged. Duke Bowen had been the children's friend too. He had done what he could, but no bronze marker was put up for him.

Jesus bothers us with the question. How well do we know our neighbor? our friends? We are told we live in a world of lonely people. Jesus found them wherever he went. But he reached out to them because he loved them, just as the policeman saw an opportunity to safeguard the lives of children on a busy street corner, so can we reach out and help others to make it safely through life. Be a friend today.

Someday You'll Understand

"I waited patiently for the Lord; and he inclined
unto me, and heard my cry."
Psalm 40:1

The writer of the Psalms must have fallen into deep sorrow. He uses strong words when he talks to God and tells him how he was brought up from a horrible pit, "out of the miry clay, and set . . . upon a rock" (Ps. 40:2). And then he makes his salvation complete when he adds, "He hath put a new song in my mouth" (Ps. 40:3).

People are always talking about values. The teacher who tries to instill honesty, faith, loyalty, belief in self to his pupils. Parents who tenderly guide children into adulthood. There are so many people who are involved in values.

Russel Sanders was my third-grade teacher. He was thin and tall. He came from a farm so poor it would barely grow wild raspberry bushes. He drove a horse to an old buggy and stabled it in the woodshed at school.

I never knew a man more kind and gentle. He took special pains to teach us about the bugs and the birds, common to all country children. Frequently we had a bird with a broken wing in a box at school. Russel Sanders could set a bird's broken wing so well that when we released it in the schoolyard, it flew away.

I think he was the poorest boy I ever knew. He would teach a year and then go back to school. He was thirty years old when he got his degree from college. By that time he was making eight hundred dollars a year and driving a Model T Ford to the town school. Russel Sanders kept on reaching for an impossible dream. And then at the age of thirty-eight he held in his hand his medical degree. It had been a long journey, long years of working and waiting and maybe long years of discouragement and loneliness and defeat.

The man who had helped so many children in the schoolroom at last turned to his chosen field of medicine. It had been an impossible dream, but he had joined the ranks of the great women and great men of this country who achieved although there were great odds against them.

God has a lesson for us. We work a lifetime and then in what seems to be the prime of life, we slip away from this world. It must be this way. All things that have a beginning must have an end, except that which belongs to God. The rains come, the morning comes, the night comes, the trees blossom and leaf and the fruit comes and the leaves fall. What about man? What is God's plan for him? He makes it clear that for man there is a passing into eternal life. And there man lives with the spirit and knowledge that he has acquired in his lifetime.

It was in 1916 that Russel Sanders stepped into the one room school for the first time as a teacher. Yet the spirit of his life, the spirit of inquiry, the spirit of faith, the spirit of life in all its greatness that he instilled in the children he taught, is remembered.

What Do You Want Me to Do, God?

"Study to shew thyself approved unto God, a
workman that needeth not to be ashamed, rightly
dividing the word of truth."
2 Timothy 2:15

Martha Wilson never went beyond the fourth grade in a
country school. She was married when she was fifteen. She
could milk a cow, dress a chicken, make good soda biscuits,
examine the ears of her children to see if they were clean
before she sent them to school.

One of her common sayings was, "Now take a bath and
put on clean stockings." When her children protested that
they were only going to town she would say, "What if you
got sick and had to go to the hospital?"

None of her children ever had to go to the hospital. All
that scrubbing for nothing. But Martha Wilson knew that
the hospital was only for the few. She wasn't content to just
milk cows and care for a family of four children. Had she
lived fifty years later she might have gone to college and become a teacher or maybe a United States Senator.

Martha Wilson had a mind of her own. And although the
four years of schooling was all she ever had, when she died
at the age of eighty-nine, many people her children did not
know came to her funeral and letters by the dozen came in
from all over the United States. All of these people had something special in common with Martha Wilson.

The closest doctor from her farm was four miles away.
He covered a territory of five miles in all directions from
Centerville, driving his horse to the homes where he was
needed. Babies were often born before he got there and sometimes died at birth. When he did get there, he usually made

out a bill for ten or fifteen dollars. Sometimes he was away from the office as much as four hours, and many times in the middle of the night.

Martha Wilson was angry one day when she went to the funeral of Bessie Smith, a beautiful young woman of twenty who died in childbirth because the doctor was not there. She went to the doctor and asked for help. She rode around the countryside with the doctor in his buggy and learned that seldom did a baby or mother die when the doctor was present. The doctor taught her not only how to become a successful midwife but also how to help mothers limit the number of children they had.

Martha Wilson's black bag was a blue granite washpan, holding inside a spool of thread, sharp scissors, a needle and thread, several pads of cloth, a bottle of alcohol, and if money permitted it—the luxury of cotton pads.

It wasn't long after her telephone rang that the neighbors would see her going down the road in her buggy with a cloud of dust behind her. She never lost a baby. She was sad when a mother died because of poison in the system she could not help.

And those who remembered her when she passed to the other side of life were the men and women that Martha Wilson had helped to bring into the world.

God Answers Prayer

If you have ever been to Grand Pre, the historic village in Kings County on Minas Basin, you have walked to the churchyard and looked upon the statue of Evangeline, the woman who searched a lifetime to find Gabriel, the man she loved.

At the end of Queen Ann's War in 1713, Acadia was given to the English. Because the French people who lived there would not take the oath of allegiance to the king of England, the Acadians were forced to leave their homes. It was in the churchyard that the orders of banishment were read.

Many of the French families settled in Louisiana, but many of them became separated on the long journey. Gabriel and Evangeline had celebrated their engagement to be married before banishment from Acadia. On the journey by rafts down the Mississippi the two lovers became separated. With hope gone of finding the man she loved, Evangeline joined the Sisters of Mercy and devoted her life to others. She found Gabriel many years later when he was about to die.

Sometimes you feel that God has forgotten you. Life is a time of struggle, a time of dreaming, a time of loving. You walk with wonder through the woods in the spring when the wildflowers seem to spring from the earth. You thrill when a child curls his fingers around yours. You stand proud when you are presented with a pin for service as a Sunday School teacher or you get a standing ovation for successfully coaching a club play.

There are many rewards in life. Phyllis Bradley said the other day, "Oh, yes, I visit the nursing home here in my town every week, taking cookies to the patients, sometimes flowers, but I always find time to stop and talk and care for these people. How do I do it? I always say a prayer when my visit is over and I can walk out the front door. They can't."

What Evangeline felt in losing the man she loved has been felt by people everywhere, the loss of someone dear. God does hear prayers. He does answer. Sometimes it is not always the answer we want. Sometimes he directs us into a field of service where we find enrichment in living. But sometimes the burden must be carried.

What is a crown of life? It is joy now, today. It is in reaching out to find beauty in life. It is to be needed by another person. It is to bravely walk into the future, knowing that God is Love. A crown of life is feeling useful in one's community. It is being proud to walk down the street of your town and speak to people. It is to look at a building, an institution, a project that has a part of your life in it. It is to open a book in the children's room at the library and find your name in it, a gift that you gave.

What Shall I Do With My Life?

"Let your light so shine before men, that they
may see your good works, and glorify your Father
which is in heaven."

Matthew 5:16

"What shall I do with my life?" is not a question asked only by the person who chooses to go to college. It is asked by the man or woman who retires from a job.

To some men it may be easy. It means freedom to fish and play golf. To a woman it means continued care of a house. To a husband and wife it may mean moving to Florida into retirement. It means saying good-bye to friends and familiar scenes. To others it means time for entertaining grandchildren and time for travel.

God asks this question every day, but sometimes we are too busy to hear. But to say each morning, "What shall I do with my life today?" is to face life with joy. Joy of the unknown. Joy of achievement.

Wesley Johnson wanted to be a carpenter. He was happy with a hammer in his hand, nailing a board on the fence, making a bookcase for his room. He liked the touch and smell of wood. But he had no choice what he would do with his life. His father had decided that. There would be no carpenter in the family. Wesley Johnson would go to medical school and become a doctor and join his father in practice. A doctor was a respected man in the community, and Wesley had it made clear to him that it would be medical school or nothing.

Wesley became a doctor. He invited me to his house one day. It was a rambling white brick that spoke of wealth, prestige, success. Wesley Johnson had become all his father wanted him to be, a successful surgeon, a family man in the community, a member of three community boards.

I was introduced to the wife, three children, and the English setter, then taken for a tour of the basement. I gave a low whistle before I reached the bottom steps. In a fine highly polished workshop of pine paneling were beautiful pieces of furniture. There were lamps, stools, a cedar chest, two bookcases, baskets, some in walnut and cherry and maple.

"Twelve-months work," Wesley proudly said, as he showed me the wood-working machines, the power tools of his shop. "Christmas presents," he added. "I really enjoy giving them to my friends—something I've made with my hands."

He told me about his work as a doctor. "But you know, Frank, I never got the idea out of my mind of wanting to be a carpenter. I don't have much time, but I don't play golf and I don't fish. I spend a lot of time playing croquet and swimming with my family in our backyard pool, but when I do have the time, I am down here if only for an hour a day and on weekends."

Wesley Johnson has a story for many, many who work at jobs they do not like but keep because the job supports the family. This does not mean that dreams must die. There is always a place to reach out and grow and have fun.

A Cabin in the Moonlight

"Your old men shall dream dreams, your young
men shall see visions."
Joel 2:28

Who has not yearned for a cabin in the moonlight, a cabin on a mountainside far from automobiles, the computer, the timeclock, the stress and tension of living?

It does not have to be a fancy cabin. Just a low one with a door and a window and a fireplace and marigolds blooming around the path to the door. There will be sun on the blue lake in the morning. In the cool of the evening, blue smoke will curl from the stone chimney. The blue smoke drifts slowly into the air, not in a hurry to get away.

Who has not dreamed of sitting before a cabin door watching the sun in the late afternoon painting the sky as it dips towards the timberline?

And sometimes when the air is cool and one sits before the blazing logs in the fireplace, perhaps there can be seen a face framed with golden hair, a red scarf, or some such memory of long ago for the old, of the future for the young.

And maybe there will be a walk out into the moonlight with the sound of ducks honking overhead, the hoot of an owl in some faraway tree.

To dream! To reach out and tell the world to stand still so that you can get off. No mailbox to go to, no telephone to answer, no board meeting to attend. The luxury of dreaming for just a little while, walking into a wilderness to a cabin beside a lake with soft winds in the white pines at night to sing you to sleep.

Only a dream. The hospital needs you on the nursing floor.

A boy needs you for a Scout trip. A busy farmer needs you to repair his tractor, a child needs you in the classroom, a retirement home needs you to drive the truck carrying hot meals. There are so many needs.

Cabin in the mountains. You are my place of prayer. You are an altar for my soul. You bring me close to the earth, to the trees, to the flowing stream, to the meadows of flowers. You help me to find myself again, to renew my soul and my body so that I can go back. I love you, but I know I must go back. I must always go back.

And so I say good-bye to you. The ashes in the fireplace are cold. There was frost on the roof this morning. Soon the winds will bring the snows and the door will be drifted shut. The birds will be gone, the bear in hibernation, and there will be the lonely howl of the wolves across the frozen lake.

I take one last look as I go down the trail. I want to hold in my memory the sound of rain upon the roof, the company of the stars and the moon, the night calls of the wild. I know I must go back to the ringing of my telephone and to the bills that the postman brings, and to people that I love.

Men Shall Live by Faith

"Behold, his soul which is lifted up is not upright
in him: but the just shall by his faith."
Habakkuk 2:4

Many years ago in a white frame house in Abilene, Kansas, a young boy lay in his bed crying. He knew that the doctor was on his way to amputate his leg which was in a state of gangrene poisoning. But God spoke to Dwight D. Eisenhower and the tears turned to a determination that it was not meant to be that he go through life with one leg.

He posted his brother outside the bedroom door with a plea that the doctor not be allowed to pass. His brother turned the doctor away and the boy survived who was to become a commander of operations in Europe and the president of the United States.

Today one may walk through the typical middle-class home of a half century or more ago, a home with its upright piano, the mohair living room furniture, the big high-posted wooden beds, and the family kitchen where Ike and his brothers gathered for so many family meals in an atmosphere of love.

Only a half block away in a small chapel this great American lies today. It is doubtful if any American received more honor than Dwight D. Eisenhower as his funeral train made its way slowly to the town where Eisenhower grew up.

Do the great become great because of a dream? Were they dreamers who crossed the mountains, the rivers, felled the forests, plowed up the grass, built churches and schools and cities? Was the yearning for a new land and opportunity the same that was in the heart of Abraham when he heard the voice of God telling him to go and build a new nation?

God is ever with us. Man goes on his way unlocking the secrets of the world, discoving God's laws, yet feeling in all his accomplishments the hand of God's love and God's guidance.

It is by faith that two young people walk side by side into life. It is by faith that a child goes to school and learns to use his mind. It is by faith that hospitals and youth centers are built. It is by faith that men gather at the United Nations and work for peace. It is by faith that a man works long hours at the test tubes unlocking the secrets of disease.

Without a challenge life has no worth. To have discovered all things, to have gained the world is to have lost one's life. You will never really know yourself, the potential you have for greatness, for service, for achievement.

You cannot separate the words *faith* and *dream* because they are so much alike. All that men have ever accomplished in the world began as a dream. All that man ever did was because he had faith that he could.

It is time to relearn the art of looking up.